The Symphony Of Struggle

A Journey Through Life's Discordant Notes

Aksa Shafi

BookLeaf Publishing

India | USA | UK

Made with ❤ on the BookLeaf Publishing Platform
www.bookleafpub.in
www.bookleafpub.com

Dedication

"To the person I was yesterday, the person I am today, and the person I will become tomorrow - may these words serve as a reminder that growth is a journey, not a destination, and that every step forward is a step closer to becoming the best version of ourselves."

Preface

To the ones who dare to dream, even when life feels like an uphill battle.

To my parents, who taught me the meaning of perseverance and unconditional love, and to every teacher who believed in me when I doubted myself.

To the sleepless nights, the overwhelming fears, and the quiet victories—thank you for shaping me into who I am today.

And to anyone out there chasing a dream that feels impossibly far away: this is for you. You are not alone. Keep going.

Acknowledgements

I stand on the shoulders of my own resilience and determination, and I am deeply grateful for the journey that has led me to this moment. This book is a testament to the power of perseverance, hard work, and the willingness to learn and grow.

I would like to express my heartfelt gratitude to those who have supported me along the way. To my parents, for their love and encouragement; to those who discouraged me, thank you for teaching me to fight my demons and discover my inner strength; and to Bookleaf Publications, thank you for your unwavering belief in my vision and for bringing this book to life. Your insights, patience, and guidance have been invaluable.

I also acknowledge the quiet moments of self-doubt and the loud moments of triumph, for they have both shaped me into the writer I am today. The late nights, early mornings, and countless hours spent researching, writing, and editing have been a transformative experience. Finally, to you, the reader: thank you for allowing my words to be part of your journey. This book is a labor of love, born from my passions and insights. May it inspire, motivate, and resonate with you, and serve as a comforting reminder that you are not alone.

Sincerely,
Aksa Shafi

1. "The Present: A Gift of Endless Possibilities"

In the tapestry of time, a thread is spun,
The present moment, where possibilities are won.
A crossroads of choice, where paths converge and meet,
The present is a canvas, where our futures are uniquely
sweet.

Like a blank page waiting for words to be penned,
The present invites us to author our own end.
A chance to rewrite the stories of our past,
To heal the wounds and let love forever last.

In this fleeting instant, we hold the power to choose,
To shape our destinies and let our spirits cruise.
The present is a gift wrapped in uncertainty,
A mystery waiting to unfold with each new possibility.

Like a river flowing, ever-changing and free,
The present moment carries us to our destiny.
With every breath, a new chance unfolds,

To create, to dream, to love, and to grow old.

So let us seize this moment with hearts full of cheer,
And turn the possibilities into a brighter year.
For in the present's promise, we find the power to create,
A future that's worthy of our highest aspirations' weight.

In the present's light, our true selves are revealed,
Our strengths and weaknesses, our passions and our
zeal.
A chance to rediscover, to recharge and renew,
To find our purpose and our meaning, and to see it
through.

Like a masterpiece unfolding, with every brushstroke
bold,
The present moment paints a picture, yet untold.
A story of hope and resilience, of trials and of strife,
A testament to the human spirit, and its capacity for life.

So let us cherish this moment, and hold it dear,
For in its possibilities, our true potential appears.
And as we step into the unknown, with hearts full of
faith,
We'll find that the present moment is the greatest gift of
all, in every way.

2. "Time's Relentless Tide"

Though you may stand still, unmoving and strong,
Change will come, and your world will be rearranged, all
day long.
Like the river's flow, it will carve its own way,
Leaving the familiar behind, come what may.

The seasons will turn, and the winds will shift and sway,
Bringing new life to some and taking it away from
others each day.
The earth will spin round, and the stars will realign,
Reminding us that change is the only constant that's
truly divine.

You may try to hold on to what's familiar and dear,
But like sand between fingers, it will slip away and
disappear.
For change is the engine that drives life's grand design,
And though you may stand still, it will keep on moving,
all the time.

So let go of the fear and the uncertainty too,
And learn to flow with the changes, like a river flowing
anew.
For in the end, it's not the standing still that will set you
free,
But the courage to move forward, wild and carefree.

And when the winds of change blow strong and wild and
wide,
And you're forced to step into the unknown, with a heart
full of pride,
Remember that change is the catalyst that will set your
soul on fire,
And though you may stand still, it will keep on moving,
and never tire.

3. "A Prayer for Freedom"

May you find the freedom to let go,
To release the need for a specific outcome to show.
May you learn to trust in the universe's plan,
And find peace in the present, hand in hand.

My greatest hope for you is that you'll find
The courage to say, "The outcome is not mine."
May you be brave enough to surrender and let be,
And find joy in the journey, wild and carefree.

For when you release the need for control,
You'll find a sense of peace that you've never known
before.
You'll be able to flow like a river to the sea,
Unencumbered by worries, wild and carefree.

You'll learn to trust the currents of life,
And find that they carry you to new heights and new
experiences in strife.
You'll discover that the journey is the destination,

And that the present moment is the only true creation.

So may you reach this point, dear one, I pray,
Where the outcome doesn't matter, and you're free to
play.
May you dance in the moment, with abandon and glee,
And find joy in the journey, wild and carefree.

May you find the strength to let go of fear,
And trust that the universe has your back, always near.
May you learn to listen to your heart's deep voice,
And follow its guidance, with courage and joyful choice.

May you remember that life is a journey, not a test,
And that every moment is a gift, to be cherished and
blessed.
May you find the wisdom to trust in the unknown,
And the courage to take the next step, into the unknown.

4. "I'll Walk My Path Alone"

I'll never ask for a helping hand
My pride and strength, I'll take my stand
I'll face my struggles, my trials, and strife
And I'll emerge stronger, with a heart full of life

But though I'll never ask, I'll always recall
Those who offered aid, who stood tall
Their kindness and compassion, I'll never forget
And though I didn't take it, their offer I'll always respect

Their words of encouragement, their listening ear
Their willingness to help, though I didn't come near
These acts of kindness will stay with me always
And though I'll walk my path alone, I'll remember their
ways

I'll remember those who saw me struggle and fall
And though I refused their help, they stood by me
through it all
Their presence was a reminder that I'm not alone

A comforting feeling that I've never known

So let this be a lesson to all who can see
That even though I may not ask, I'm grateful for your
generosity
And though I'll walk my path alone, I'll never forget
Those who offered help and showed me they cared and
didn't forget

Their selflessness and kindness are a beacon in the night
A guiding light that shines so bright
It illuminates the path and shows me the way
And though I'll walk alone, I'll never stray

For in their kindness, I've found a strength
A resolve to keep moving forward, at any length
To face my challenges, to overcome my fears
And though I'll walk my path alone, I'll wipe away my
tears

So here's to those who offered help and showed they care
Though I may not have taken it, I'll always remember
they were there
And though I'll walk my path alone, I'll never forget
The kindness of strangers and the love they've beget.

5. "In the Moments of Darkness"

When shadows creep and doubts arise
And fears and worries fill your eyes
Remember in the dark of night
You are a star, a shining light

Your worth is not defined by strife
But by the strength that helps you thrive
In every test, in every fall
You've risen up, and stood through it all

Don't let the darkness make you forget
The beauty, love, and light you've met
The kindness that has touched your soul
The love that makes you whole

You are a warrior, brave and true
A survivor of all that you've been through
Your scars are proof of your strength and might
A reminder that you've made it through the night

So when the darkness closes in
And you feel lost, and can't begin
To find your way, or see the light
Remember your worth, and hold on tight

You are enough, just as you are
A unique and precious gem, a shining star
Don't let the darkness make you forget
Your worth, your value, and the love you've met

Remember the moments that made your heart sing
The laughter, the joy, the love that makes you whole
Remember the people who stood by your side
The ones who lifted you up, and helped you to abide

Remember the strength that lies within your soul
The resilience, the courage, that makes you whole
Remember the love you've received and given
The kindness, the compassion, that you've lived and
striven

So when the darkness closes in, and you feel lost and
alone
Just remember the light that shines within your soul
It's the spark of your spirit, the fire that burns bright
A reminder of your worth, on even the darkest night

You are a shining star that twinkles in the night
A beacon of hope that shines with all your might
You are a precious gem that sparkles with delight
A treasure to behold, a wonder to excite

So hold on to your worth, and never let it go
Remember the light that shines within your soul
It's the spark of your spirit, the fire that burns bright
A reminder of your worth, on even the darkest night.

6. "What is Meant for You"

What is meant for you will find its way
Through the twists and turns of life's busy day
It will seek you out and gently come to stay
And in its presence, you'll find your heart's own way

What is meant for you will not be delayed
It will arrive in time and never be swayed
By the doubts and fears that may assail your mind
For what is meant for you is forever intertwined

With the threads of fate and the whispers of the heart
It will guide you forward and never depart
Through the darkness and the light, it will be your guide
And lead you to the place where you'll reside

What is meant for you will not be taken away
It will be yours to keep, come what may
So trust in the universe and its gentle hand
For what is meant for you will forever stand

In the stillness of the night, when stars shine bright
Listen to the whispers of your heart and its gentle light
For it will lead you to the place where your dreams come
true
And what is meant for you will be waiting there for you

Do not be fooled by doubts and fears that may try to lead
you astray
For what is meant for you will always find its way
Through the noise and the chaos, it will whisper your
name
And guide you to the place where your heart will find its
flame

So trust in the universe and its plan for your life
For what is meant for you will always be your guide
And when the darkness closes in, and you feel lost and
alone
Just remember, what is meant for you will always find its
way back home.

7. "If It Costs Me My Peace"

If it costs me my peace, then it has to go
A price too high to pay, I must let it show
That my serenity is worth more than gold
And I won't sacrifice it, no matter how bold

The noise, the chaos, the stress, and the fray
If they disrupt my calm, then they must go away
I won't be held hostage by the demands of the day
My peace is my priority, come what may

The relationships that drain me, the ones that bring me
pain
If they cost me my peace, then I must walk away, in vain
No amount of love or loyalty can make me stay
If my serenity is compromised, then I must seize the day

The fears, the doubts, the worries that creep in at night
If they cost me my peace, then I must shine a light
On the truth that sets me free, on the love that makes me
whole

And let go of the anxiety that takes its toll

The expectations, the pressures, the weights that I bear
If they cost me my peace, then I must show I care
For my own well-being, for my own heart's sake
I'll let go of the burdens that my peace would undertake

The world outside may be loud, wild, and free
But in my inner world, I'll cultivate serenity
A garden of peace, where love and joy reside
Where my heart can heal, and my spirit can abide

If it costs me my peace, then it has to go
I'll choose serenity over strife and let my spirit glow
In the stillness and the calm, I'll find my peaceful nest
And nothing will disturb me; I'll be at rest

So I'll let go of the things that disturb my peace
And hold on to the love that my heart release
I'll trust in the universe and its plan for my life
And know that my peace is worth more than any strife.

8. "Forgiving the Unrepentend"

Forgiving someone who isn't sorry is not easy to do
It takes a heart that's willing, and a soul that's true
To let go of the hurt, and the pain they've caused
To release the burden of resentment, and the weight of
the pause

It's hard to forgive when they don't acknowledge their
wrong
When they don't apologize, or show any sign of being
strong
It's hard to let go when the wound is still so fresh
When the memories of the hurt are still so deeply etched

Their silence is deafening, their indifference a test
But I won't let their actions define me, I won't let them
be my guest
I'll rise above the hurt, I'll shine above the pain
And I'll find my own way, my own path to forgiveness
and gain

But forgiveness is not for them, it's for me
It's for my own healing, my own liberty
It's for the peace that I crave, the peace that I need
To move on from the hurt, and to plant a new seed

Forgiveness is a journey, a path that's long and slow
It's a process of letting go, of releasing the weight that I
know
It's a choice that I make every day, every hour, every
minute too
To forgive, to let go, and to find my peace anew

So I'll choose to forgive, though it's hard to do
I'll choose to let go, and to see this through
I'll choose to release the pain, and the weight of the past
And to find my own peace, my own healing at last

I'll learn to love myself, to care for my own heart
To nurture my own soul, and to play a brand new part
I'll rise above the hurt, I'll shine above the pain
And I'll find my own way, my own path to forgiveness
and gain

Forgiving someone who isn't sorry is not easy, I know
But it's a step towards healing, a step towards letting go
It's a step towards peace, towards freedom and release

And it's a step that I'll take, with courage and with ease.

9. "If I Ever Needed You"

If I ever needed you, and you weren't there
I'll never need you again, I swear
The moment I reached out, and you turned away
Was the moment I realized, I'd be okay

I thought our bond was strong, our trust unbreakable
But in that moment, I felt my heart unshakable
The pain of your absence, the weight of your neglect
It was a burden I couldn't bear, a wound I couldn't
correct

I searched for answers, for reasons why
You weren't there for me, when I needed you to try
But the silence was deafening, the emptiness a test
And I knew in that moment, I had to let go of the rest

If I ever needed you, and you weren't there
I'll never need you again, I swear
I'll find my own way, I'll heal my own heart
And I'll learn to love myself, to never depart

From that moment on, I knew I'd be just fine
I'd find my own strength, my own voice, my own rhyme
I'd rise above the hurt, I'd shine above the pain
And I'd never again rely on someone who couldn't
remain

I'll take care of myself, I'll be my own best friend
I'll learn to love and trust myself, until the very end
I'll find my own happiness, my own sense of pride
And I'll never again settle for someone who couldn't be
by my side

If I ever needed you, and you weren't there
I'll never need you again, I swear
I'll move on with my life, I'll find my own way
And I'll never look back, come what may

The memories of our past, they will slowly fade
And I'll be left with the knowledge, that I'm better off
without the shade
Of someone who couldn't be there, when I needed them
most
And I'll be grateful for the lesson, that I learned from the
ghost

Of a relationship that's lost, of a love that's gone cold

But I'll rise above the ashes, like a phoenix, bold
I'll find my own way, I'll heal my own heart
And I'll never again need someone, who couldn't play
their part.

10. "I Made It and I'm Still Here"

I've walked through fire, and I've faced the rain
I've been broken, shattered, and driven to pain
But I'm still standing, still breathing, still alive
I made it through the darkness, and I survived

I've been to the depths of my own despair
I've seen the shadows that lurk, and the demons that
stare
But I've faced them head-on, with a heart that's bold
And I've risen above them, like a phoenix from the cold

I've made mistakes, and I've stumbled and fell
But I've gotten back up, and I've learned to yell
I've found my voice, and I've spoken my truth
And I've risen above the noise, with a heart that's youth

I've been through the storm, and I've weathered the
night

*I've seen the darkest moments, and I've held on to the
light*
I've been broken, but I've been remade
And I'm stronger now, with a heart that's not afraid

I'm still here, still standing, still strong and free
*I've made it through the struggles, and I've learned to be
me*
*I've found my own way, through the darkness and the
light*
*And I'm still shining, still burning, like a beacon in the
night*

I've learned to love myself, to care for my own soul
*I've learned to heal my own heart, and to make myself
whole*
I've learned to stand up tall, to face my fears with pride
*And I've learned to rise above, with a heart that won't be
denied*

I made it, and I'm still here
A warrior, a survivor, a soul that's clear
I've been through the fire, and I've been through the rain
*But I'm still standing, still alive, still rising above the
pain*

I'll keep on walking, I'll keep on standing tall

I'll keep on shining, I'll keep on rising above it all
I'll keep on being me, with a heart that's strong and free
And I'll keep on rising, like a phoenix, wild and carefree.

11. "Patience's Reward"

What we deserve takes time to grow,
A garden of dreams, where seeds must sow.
We plant with care, with hope, and with might,
And wait for the harvest, under starry night.

The universe works at its own sweet pace,
Guiding us forward with a gentle, loving face.
It weaves a tapestry of trials and strife,
But in the end, it's worth it for the beauty of life.

So let's not rush through the journey we take,
For what we deserve is worth the wait we make.
Let's trust the process and have faith in the plan,
For in the end, we'll receive what we've been working to
hand.

The best things in life are those that take their time,
Like a fine wine aging or a sunrise that climbs.
So let's be patient and let our dreams unfold,
For what we deserve will be worth more than gold.

12. "A Broken Tear"

A single tear, a shattered dream
A heart once whole, now broken it seems
The pain of loss, the sting of sorrow
A tear that falls, a heart that borrows

Memories of joy, now taunt and tease
A bittersweet reminder of what could never be
The weight of grief, the ache of longing
A tear that falls, a heart that's wronged

In the silence, I hear your voice
A whispered promise, a haunting choice
To hold on tight, or let go and fall
A broken tear, a heart that loses all

I search for answers, in the dark of night
For a glimmer of hope, a shining light
To guide me through, the stormy sea
And lead me back, to a heart that's free

But like a ghost, you haunt me still
A fleeting shadow, a lingering chill
That sends shivers down, my spine so fine
And leaves me trembling, with a heart that's mine

Yet even in darkness, a light will shine
A glimmer of hope, a heart that's mine
A chance to heal, to mend and to repair
A broken heart, a tear that's dried with care

And though it's hard, to let go of the pain
I'll learn to love again, to live and to sustain
The memories of you, the joy and the tears
And find a way, to calm my doubts and fears

For time will heal, the wounds of my heart
And though it's broken, it will never depart
For it's a part of me, a piece of my soul
A broken tear, a heart that's made whole.

13. "Silent Souls"

In the stillness, I find my peace,
A world outside that my soul can't release,
The chaos, the noise, the constant din,
Are silenced by the quiet within.

Going silent is my comfort zone,
Where I can breathe, and be alone,
No need for words, no need to explain,
Just the quiet calm, the stillness that remains.

In this space, I find my strength,
A refuge from the world's loud length,
Where I can recharge, and renew my soul,
And find the courage to make myself whole.

So let me be still, let me be quiet too,
For in the silence, I find my peace anew,
It's not that I'm shy, or that I'm afraid,
It's just that silence is where my heart is made.

In the quiet, I hear my own voice,
A whisper of wisdom, a heartfelt choice,
To step back, observe, and truly see,
The world around me, in all its glee.

The silence is my sanctuary, my nest,
Where I can rest, and be at my best,
No distractions, no noise, no fray,
Just the peaceful silence, every single day.

So I'll cherish this silence, this quiet space,
Where I can find myself, and my own pace,
For in the stillness, I am free to be,
My authentic self, wild and carefree.

14. "Notice Who's Too Busy"

Notice who's too busy for you,
But finding time for others, is true.
Their schedule is full, or so they claim,
But they'll make time for those they deem worthy of
their fame.

They'll cancel plans, or ignore your call,
But for others, they'll give their all.
They'll make excuses, or simply disappear,
Leaving you wondering, if you're worthy to hold dear.

But don't take it personally, it's not about you,
It's about them, and what they can do.
They're building their empire, or so they think,
But in the process, they're leaving relationships to sink.

So notice who's too busy for you,
But finds time for others, it's true.
And know your worth, don't wait around,
For those who don't value you, will only let you down.

Invest in those who invest in you,
And don't waste time on those who don't see your value
true.
You deserve better, don't settle for less,
Notice who's too busy, and let them be the rest.

15. "Heartbeat of Self"

You are here for yourself, a truth so divine
A path unwinding, where self-love will shine
In the midst of chaos, remember to breathe
You are the anchor that holds yourself free

Your heart beats for you, a rhythm so true
A symphony of self, played just for you
Don't let the world outside define your worth
You are the compass that guides yourself on this earth

You are here to heal, to grow, and to explore
To unravel the threads of self-doubt and more
To discover your strengths, passions, and inner fire
To nurture your soul and your heart's greatest desire

In the stillness of night, when stars shine bright
Listen to your whispers; your inner voice takes flight
It guides you through darkness, uncertainty, and fear
And leads you to the light, where self-love and
acceptance appear

You are here for yourself, a journey so grand
A pilgrimage of self-discovery in this land
So be kind to yourself, gentle, and true
Remember, you are here for yourself, and that's enough,
anew

Through trials and tribulations, you'll find your way
Through the noise and chaos, you'll hear your heart say
"I am enough, I am worthy, I am strong and free"
And when you do, you'll know you're exactly where
you're meant to be

You are the architect of your life's design
The author of your story, the hero of your mind
Write your own narrative with courage and heart
And shine with delight, a love that will never depart.

16. "Emptied Cups"

I once poured my heart and soul,
Into cups that never made me whole.
I gave and gave without a care,
But received only emptiness and air.

Their depths seemed bottomless, it seemed,
No matter how much I poured, they gleamed.
But never once did they refill,
Leaving me drained, with a hollow will.

But then I learned to let go,
To stop pouring into cups that didn't glow.
I saved my love, my time, and my tears,
And found that life had more to offer through the years.

Now my cup overflows with love,
From those who give as much as they receive,
And pour it back from hearts that truly care,
And life got better with love that's fair and rare.

So let this be a lesson to all,
To pour into cups that pour back, standing tall.
For when we give to those who give in return,
Our lives are richer, and our hearts learn.

17. "It's Who You Are at Your Core"

Beneath the surface, where the truth resides,
Lies the essence of you, where love abides.
It's who you are at your core, where the heart meets the
soul,
A beauty that shines, making your spirit whole.

Strip away the layers, the masks you wear,
And you'll find the real you, without a single care.
It's you that's been there, through every fall,
The resilience that rises, standing tall.

It's who you are at your core, where kindness reigns,
A compassion that overflows, easing life's pains.
It's the love that you hold, the light that you share,
A treasure that's uniquely yours, beyond compare.

Don't let the world define, what's already divine,
You are enough, just as you are, in this moment's shine.
It's who you are at your core, that truly matters most,

A beauty, a love, a light, that forever will boast.

In the stillness of the night, when the world is asleep,
Listen to the whispers, of your heart's deepest keep.
It's where your truth resides, where your soul finds its
voice,
A gentle reminder, of your innermost choice.

So let go of the need, to conform and to fit,
Embrace your uniqueness, and let your spirit hit.
It's who you are at your core, that makes you shine so
bright,
A beacon of hope, in the darkest of nights.

Remember, you are more, than the sum of your parts,
A complex tapestry, woven with love and heart.
It's who you are at your core, that gives you strength and
might,
A guiding force, that leads you through life's plight.

So hold on to your core, and never let it fade,
For it's the essence of you, that makes your heart parade.
It's who you are at your core, that truly sets you free,
A beautiful, unique, and precious soul, wild and carefree.

18. "It's Worth It"

There are times when the road gets long,
And the journey seems to be going wrong,
When struggles weigh upon your chest,
And doubts creep in, making you feel unblessed.

But I'll tell you this, through every test,
It's worth it—every step, every quest,
For in the fire, you're refined and made
Stronger, wiser, with a heart that's not afraid.

The darkness fades; the light will shine,
And you'll emerge with a spirit that's divine,
The battles won, the lessons learned,
Will guide you on as your heart yearns.

So hold on tight; don't let go,
For the prize is worth it; don't you know?
The joy, the peace, the love you'll find
Will be worth every tear, every struggle left behind.

It's worth it—every step of the way,
Through every stormy night to a brighter day,
So keep on walking; don't lose your stride,
For the reward is worth it, deep inside.

When the world outside is cold and gray,
And fears and worries come to stay,
Just remember, you're not alone,
For every step forward is a victory to own.

The journey's not easy, but it's worth the fight,
For in the end, you'll shine with all your might,
Your heart will heal; your soul will mend,
And you'll emerge stronger, with a story to lend.

So don't give up; don't lose your way,
For every step forward is a brighter day,
It's worth it—every struggle, every fall,
For in the end, you'll rise above it all

19. "The Pages Will Keep Turning"

As one chapter ends, another begins,
A new story unfolds with its own twists and spins.
The pages will keep turning, don't you know?
A fresh start awaits with a story yet untold.

Memories of yesterday will forever remain,
But the future beckons with its own joy and pain.
The pages will turn with each passing day,
A new chapter unfolds in a brand new way.

So let go of the past with its triumphs and fears,
And step into the unknown through laughter and tears.
The pages will keep turning with every breath you take,
A new chapter begins for your heart to make.

In this new chapter, may you find your way,
Through life's ups and downs in a brighter day.
May your heart be filled with love and delight,
As the pages turn into a brand new light.

So here's to the next chapter in this story of yours,
May it be filled with wonder and a heart that endures.
The pages will keep turning, and a new chapter will begin,
A fresh start awaits with a story yet to win.

20. "Gentle Hands"

Be gentle with others, it's true,
For everyone's fighting, with struggles anew.
Their hearts are fragile, like glass so fine,
And weary souls, with burdens that entwine.

A careless word, a thoughtless deed,
Can shatter dreams, and plant a painful seed.
So let your words be soft, and your touch be kind,
And show compassion, to the hearts and minds.

Be gentle with strangers, and gentle with friends,
For we're all connected, until the very end.
In a world that's harsh, cold, and gray,
Be a beacon of kindness, every single day.

Let empathy guide you, and compassion be your creed,
For gentle hands and hearts, are all we need.
So hold the door open, for the one behind,
And offer a smile, to the stranger you find.

Listen with an open heart, to the story they tell,
And be present in the moment, with a love that's real to
sell.
For gentle moments, we find a peaceful place,
Where love and kindness reign, and fill the space.

So let your gentleness, be a guiding light,
That shines for all to see, in the darkest night.
And when the world outside, seems loud and wild and
free,
Be a gentle soul, who brings peace and serenity.

For in the end, it's not the loud, boastful deeds,
That makes a lasting impact, but gentle words and noble
needs.

21. "Beyond the Preview"

I crave the depths, the unseen pages,
Where hearts are bared, and souls engage.
But casual talk, a fleeting glance,
Leaves me yearning for a deeper dance.

The previews end, the curtains draw,
And I'm left wanting, with an unfulfilled law.
The surface-level chatter, a mere disguise,
Conceals the richness, the untold surprise.

I long to delve, to explore and roam,
In the uncharted territories of the heart's home.
To find the hidden truths, the unspoken fears,
And in the silence, wipe away my tears.

But small talk reigns, a monarch of the land,
And I'm left searching, with an outstretched hand.
For someone who'll dive, into the unknown sea,
And with me, navigate the depths of humanity.

In a world of sound bites, and curated tales,
I yearn for authenticity, for hearts that prevail.
For in vulnerability, we find the real,
And in openness, our true selves reveal.

So let us venture, beyond the shallow end,
And in the mysteries, our true selves amend.
For in the unexplored, we'll find what's real,
And in the depths, our hearts will truly feel.

Let us exchange the masks we wear,
For the beauty of imperfection, and the love we share.
For in the depths of connection, we'll find our way,
And in the darkness, a brighter dawn will stay.

22. "The Voice of Reason"

In the realm of truth, where shadows roam
A tale unfolds, with multiple homes
Two voices whisper, with words so bright
Each one convinced, of their own light

But wisdom's whisper warns, "Do not be swayed"
By emotions or biases that have stayed
Listen deeply to both sides of the tale
Lest you judge wrongly, and justice fail

The first voice speaks with passion's fire
Convincing words that touch the heart's desire
It paints a picture of right and wrong
And makes you wonder where you belong

But then the second voice, with gentle breeze
Presents a different view, like a summer's ease
It reveals new facts and sheds new light
And makes you realize truth's not always in sight

The truth is hidden, like a gem in the night
Requiring patience and an open heart's light
To listen, to weigh, to consider with care
Both sides of the story, before a conclusion is shared

In the silence between the words we hear
Lies the truth, waiting to appear
So let us listen with hearts and minds open wide
To both sides of the story, before we decide

In this way, we'll find the truth will be revealed
And justice will be served, with hearts that are healed
For listening to both sides is the key to understanding
And in the end, it's the truth that will be standing

Through the noise and the fray, we'll find our way
To a place of clarity, where truth shines each day
And though it may take time and patience may be tried
We'll emerge with wisdom, like a morning sunrise high.

23. "The Quiet Life"

In solitude, I find my peaceful nest
A world away from the unrest of prying eyes
No interest in anyone's strife
I breathe, I live, I thrive in this quiet life

The world outside may spin and sway
But I remain unmoved, in my own way
No drama, no stress, no anxious thoughts
Just the stillness of a mind that's caught

In this empty space, I find my home
Where no one's opinions can ever roam
I am the master of my own domain
Where peace and quiet are my heart's refrain

The world may see this as isolation
But I see it as liberation's foundation
From the weights that bind and the chains that tie
I am free to live life on my own terms, and to fly

I don't need validation; I don't need praise
I don't need anyone's approval to raise
My self-worth isn't tied to external fame
I am enough, just as I am, in this quiet game

The world may be loud, but I am still
A quiet observer, watching life's thrill
I don't need to participate; I don't need to play
I am content in my own way

So let the world spin round and round
I'll stay in my peaceful, quiet ground
Where nothing disturbs, and nothing is gained,
Except the stillness of a heart that's unchained

In this solitude, I find my strength
A sense of self that's not tied to length
Of relationships or friendships or fame
I am myself, and that's all I need to claim

So I'll stay in my quiet, peaceful space
Where I can breathe, where I can find my pace
Where nothing disturbs, and nothing is gained,
Except the stillness of a heart that's unchained.

24. "The Wisdom of Silence"

Sit alone, in silence and at night,
And you'll find all your answers, shining with new light.
The world outside may be loud and unclear,
But in the stillness, your heart will whisper, "Listen here."

In the quiet hours, when the world is asleep,
You'll find the wisdom that your soul has been seeking to
keep.
The distractions will fade, the noise will subside,
And in solitude, you'll discover your heart's inside.

The answers you've been searching for will rise to the
surface,
Like bubbles in a pond, they'll gently emerge and
disperse.
The confusion will clear, the doubts will fade away,
And in the silence, you'll find a new path to slay.

So sit alone and let the stillness envelop you,
Like a warm blanket, it will comfort and renew.

Your mind, heart, and soul will find their peaceful nest,
And in solitude, you'll discover your true best.

For in the quiet hours, you'll find your inner voice,
A whisper that guides you through life's joys and
choices.
So sit alone and listen to your heart's gentle tone,
And you'll find all your answers in the silence, all your
own.

In the stillness, you'll find your strength and might,
A sense of purpose that will guide you through the
night.
You'll discover your passions, values, and goals,
And in solitude, you'll find your heart's true soul.

So don't be afraid to sit alone in the dark,
For in the silence, you'll find a spark.
A spark that will ignite, a fire that will burn,
Guiding you forward through life's twists and turns.

And when you emerge from solitude and the night,
You'll be stronger, wiser, and shining with new light.
You'll be more confident, self-assured, and bold,
And you'll find that the answers were within you all
along.

25. "The Reality of Growing Up"

We used to dream of grown-up days,
Of freedom and adventure in every way.
We'd soar on eagle's wings, untethered and free,
With the world at our feet and our hearts full of glee.

But now we're here, in this strange new land,
Where bills and responsibilities take our hand.
The world is vast, but our choices are few,
And the freedom we sought is a myth we once knew.

We thought we'd be heroes, with capes and might,
Saving the world from darkness and shining with light.
But now we're just trying to make ends meet,
And the heroes we dreamed of are just a distant beat.

We're lost in the haze of adulthood's grind,
Where the lines blur between what's real and what's
been left behind.
We're searching for answers in the dark of the night,

And the questions we asked are still echoing in our sight.

But still we hold on to the dreams of our youth,
Though they may be faded, they still shine with truth.
For in the midst of chaos, we find our own way,
And though growing up is hard, we'll face it day by day.

So we'll take a deep breath and let go of our fears,
And though the world may be more complicated than
our tears,
We'll find our own strength in the midst of the fray,
And growing up will be a journey we'll face day by day.

For in the end, it's not about the dreams we had found,
But about the journey we take to turn them into solid
ground.
And though it's not easy, and though it's not always
bright,
Growing up is a journey that's worth the fight.

We'll stumble, we'll fall, but we'll rise again,
For that's the beauty of growing up, and learning to
bend.
We'll find our own voice, our own way to be,
And though it's not perfect, it's a journey we'll see.

Through the ups and downs, the highs and the lows,

We'll find our own strength, and our own way to grow.
We'll learn to let go, to release what's past,
And find our own way, to a brighter future at last.

And when we look back, on the journey we've made,
We'll see that growing up, was a journey we've created.
With every step forward, with every fall and every rise,
We've found our own way, to a brighter, wiser surprise.

So let's take a deep breath, and let go of our fears,
And though the world may be complicated, we'll face it for years.
For growing up is a journey, that's worth the fight,
And though it's not easy, we'll shine with all our might.

26. "Heartbeats of Hope"

Your head may know the truth, but your heart may need
more time
To catch up with the wisdom that your mind has already
aligned.
It's okay to take a moment to let your emotions unfold,
For healing is a journey that can't be rushed or told.

Your heart may need to grieve, to let go of what's past,
To find its way to acceptance and learn to love again at
last.
It's okay to take the time to navigate through the pain,
For your heart is healing in its own unique way and
gain.

Don't rush the process; don't force the pace,
For your heart will find its way to a brand new place.
It's okay to take a breath, to let your emotions settle in,
For your heart is healing, and that's a journey to begin.

So be patient with yourself; be kind and gentle too,

For your heart is doing its best to heal and see this
through.
It's okay to take the time to find your way to peace,
For your heart will heal in its own unique release.

Remember, healing is not a linear line,
It's a journey with its twists and its own unique design.
So trust the process; trust your heart,
And know that healing will come in its own perfect start.

Through the darkness and the light, you'll find your way,
And though it may take time, you'll rise above the pain.
Your heart will heal; your soul will mend,
And you'll emerge stronger, with a love that will never
end.

So don't rush the healing; don't force the pace,
For your heart will find its way to a brand new place.
It's okay to take the time to navigate through the pain,
For your heart is healing, and that's a journey to obtain.

And when the darkness fades and the light begins to
shine,
You'll see that healing is a gift that's yours to design.
You'll rise above the heartache and find your way to
peace,
And your heart will heal in its own unique release.

Through the journey of healing, you'll find your inner strength,
A resilience born from trials and the length.
You'll learn to bend and flex, to adapt and endure,
And you'll find that you're capable of more than you ever knew.

So trust the process; trust your heart,
And know that healing will come in its own perfect start.
For your heart is healing in its own unique way,
And that's a journey that's yours to stay.

27. "The Power of Pain"

Let the pain be your teacher, let it guide you through,
For in its darkest moments, lies a strength anew.
Don't be afraid to face it, don't be afraid to fall,
For it's rising up again, that you'll learn to stand tall.

Let the weight of your struggles shape you like a flame,
That burns away weakness and forges a stronger frame.
Let the tears you've cried water the garden of your soul,
And let the lessons you've learned make you whole.

Don't let the pain define you, but let it refine you,
Like silver in the fire, purified and made anew.
Let it teach you to be brave, to face your deepest fears,
And to find the strength within that wipes away your
tears.

For every scar you bear is a testament to your might,
A reminder of the battles you've fought and won in the
night.

So let the pain be your teacher, let it guide you on your
way,
And you'll emerge stronger, wiser, and brighter with
each new day.

So don't be afraid of the pain, don't be afraid to hurt,
For it's in embracing your struggles that you'll find your
greatest strength and worth.
Let the pain teach you, let it shape you and mold,
And you'll rise up stronger, like a phoenix from the cold.

Through the fire and the rain, you'll find your inner
strength,
A resilience born from trials and the length.
You'll learn to bend and flex, to adapt and to endure,
And you'll find that you're capable of more than you ever
knew.

So let the pain be your catalyst for growth and
transformation,
A chance to rediscover your deepest aspirations.
Let it push you to your limits, and beyond what you can
bear,
And you'll find that you're stronger than you ever
thought you'd share.

For in the darkness, there's a light that guides you through the night,
A beacon that shines bright and leads you to the other side.
So don't be afraid of the pain, but let it be your guide,
And you'll emerge stronger, wiser, and more resilient with each stride.

28. "The Power of Authenticity"

Be a good person, with a heart so true,
But don't waste your time trying to prove it to few.
Your kindness and compassion should shine like a light,
Not to impress others, but to guide you through the
night.

Don't seek validation from those who may doubt,
Your character and integrity should speak for
themselves, without a shout.
Be humble and genuine in all that you do,
And let your actions speak louder than any words you
could pursue.

You don't need to prove yourself to anyone's eyes,
Your self-worth and value come from within, and never
compromise.
So focus on being the best version of yourself each day,
And let your authenticity shine in every single way.

Don't waste your time and energy trying to convince,
Those who may not see the goodness that you dispense.
Instead, focus on spreading love and kindness wherever
you go,
And know that your true character will forever glow.

Be a good person, not for praise or fame,
But because it's who you are, and it's the right thing to
claim.
So hold your head up high and walk with pride and
grace,
And know that your authenticity will leave a lasting
trace.

For when you're true to yourself, you'll find your inner
peace,
And your heart will be filled with joy and love that will
never cease.
So don't try to be someone you're not meant to be,
Just be yourself, and let your authenticity set you free.

And when the world tries to bring you down,
And doubts creep in, and fears wear a frown,
Just remember who you are and what you stand for,
And let your authenticity be the anchor that holds you
secure.

So be a good person, with a heart so true,
And don't waste your time trying to prove it to few.
Just be yourself, and let your authenticity shine,
And you'll find that your true character will forever be
divine.

29. "The Beauty of Being Different"

In a world that often seeks to conform,
It's easy to get lost in the norm.
But sometimes it's okay to be different, you see,
To stand out from the crowd and be unique.

Your quirks and flaws make you who you are,
A beautiful tapestry woven from near and far.
Don't try to hide them or fit into a mold,
Embracing your uniqueness is worth more than gold.

In a sea of sameness, you can be a shining light,
A beacon of individuality in the dark of night.
Your differences are what make you strong and bright,
Don't let the world dull your sparkle; let it shine with all
your might.

So don't be afraid to be yourself, to stand apart,
To celebrate your uniqueness and let your true self start.
You are a work of art, a masterpiece, one of a kind,

And the world needs more of your unique spirit, heart,
and mind.

For in a world that often values sameness and gray,
Your differences are what make you special every single
day.
So let your freak flag fly, let your true self shine,
And remember, sometimes it's okay to be different, all
the time.

Don't let the fear of judgment hold you back
From being the amazing, unique person you are, and
that's a fact.
You are a snowflake, a rare and precious find,
A one-of-a-kind masterpiece that's truly unique.

So don't try to change who you are to fit in with the
crowd,
Your uniqueness is what makes you beautiful and proud.
Embracing your differences is the key to being free,
To be the best version of yourself, as you're meant to be.

And when you're feeling lost and alone in the dark,
Just remember that your uniqueness is a spark.
A spark that can ignite, a fire that can burn,
Guiding you forward through life's twists and turns.

So let your uniqueness shine like a beacon in the night,
And remember, sometimes it's okay to be different; it's
what makes you bright.

30. "A Reflection of Time"

Time doesn't change who we are deep inside,
It only reveals the truth as the years glide.
It peels away the layers, the masks we wear,
Exposing our true selves without a single care.

At first, we may pretend and put on a show,
Hiding our true intentions as the moments flow.
But time has a way of revealing our heart's desire,
Exposing our motivations like a burning fire.

It shows us who's genuine, who's true and kind,
And who's just pretending, leaving us blind.
Time reveals the fake, the pretenders, and the cold,
And brings to light the warmth, the love that never
grows old.

So let time do its work; let it reveal and expose,
For in the end, it's not about changing, but about
disclosing.
The truth about ourselves, our intentions, and our heart,

Time will reveal it all and never depart.

For time doesn't change people; it only reveals the truth,
A reflection of our character in all its youth.
So let's not be fooled by appearances or by what we see,
For time will ultimately reveal the real you and me.

31. "Scars of Speech"

Words can cut like a knife, so sharp and so fine,
Leaving scars that never heal, a constant reminder of the
pain.
A careless phrase, a thoughtless tone, can pierce the
heart,
And leave it stone, a heavy burden to carry from the
start.

Memories of hurtful words remain, echoes of pain,
That refuse to wane, a constant ache that remains.
The wounds of words can never fade, a constant
reminder,
Of the hurt we've made, the pain we've inflicted, the
scars we've rendered.

Time may pass, but the pain stays near, a tender spot,
That's always in fear, of being hurt again, of being torn.
By the sharp edges of words that are born, of being cut,
By the knife of criticism, the dagger of doubt.

*So let us choose our words with care, and think before
we speak,*
With love to share, and kindness to seek.
For once the words are spoken, they can't be undone,
And the wounds they cause may never be won.

*For words have power, a power so great, to heal or to
hurt,*
To build or to create, to inspire or to desert.
So let us use our words to uplift and to bless,
And not to wound, or cause unnecessary stress.

*For the wounds of words can never heal, but with
kindness, love,*
*And care, we can try to reveal, a new way of speaking, a
new way of being.*
*Where words are used to heal, and not to keep on
bleeding,*
Where love and kindness are the words we're reading.

Let us be mindful of the words we say,
And think of the impact they may have each day.
Let us use our words to build each other up,
And not to tear each other down, with a careless cup.

For words have the power to make or break,
To heal or to hurt, to create or to partake.

So let us choose our words with care,
And use them to show love, kindness, and compassion
we share.

32. "Pause"

In a world that's always on the go,
Where deadlines loom and tasks seem to grow,
It's easy to get caught up in the pace,
And forget to take a moment to rest in this place.

But sometimes you have to slow down, breathe,
And let the world wait while you recharge and seize
The moment to unwind, to let your mind stray,
And find your center in a world that's gone astray.

The world will keep spinning; it won't stop or slow,
But you can, and you must, take time to let your spirit
glow.
To rest, rejuvenate, heal, and mend,
And find the strength to carry on and be your best again.

So take a step back and let the world wait;
Take time to rest and don't hesitate.
For in the stillness, you'll find your inner voice,
Guiding you forward with a heart made of choice.

*Remember, you're not a machine; you're human and
divine,*
And you deserve to rest and let your spirit shine.
So take a break and let the world spin round;
*You can always catch up when you're feeling renewed
and found.*

In a world that values productivity and speed,
It's easy to forget that rest is a vital need.
*But taking time to pause is not a sign of weakness or
fear;*
*It's a sign of strength and a willingness to listen and
hear.*

So listen to your body and listen to your soul;
*When they tell you it's time to take a break and make
whole,*
Take time to rest and don't apologize
For taking care of yourself, which is not a selfish prize.

In fact, it's a necessary act of self-love and self-care,
*That will allow you to show up with a heart that's full
and fair.*
So take a pause, breathe, and let the world slow down,
*And remember that rest is not a luxury but a necessity in
this busy town.*

33. "From Fear to Freedom."

In the depths of doubt, where shadows roam,
Fear whispers lies and makes its home.
It wraps its chains around the heart
And holds us captive, torn apart.

But on the other side of fear's dark night,
Lies a dawn of freedom, shining bright.
A world where courage blooms and love resides,
Where hearts are open and souls abide.

To reach this place, we must face the test
And walk through fire, where fears find rest.
For on the other side of fear's cold grasp,
Lies a warmth of freedom that will forever last.

So let us take the leap and step into the unknown,
Where fear's dark shadows are transformed to light
that's shown.
For on the other side of fear, we'll find our wings
And soar to heights where freedom joyfully sings.

In this realm of liberty, we'll dance and play,
Unshackled from the chains of fear's disarray.
Our hearts will beat with courage, our souls will shine so
bright,
In the radiant light of freedom's delight.

So let us not be held by fear's restrictive might,
But rise above into the freedom of light.
For on the other side of fear, we'll find our way
To a brighter tomorrow, where freedom reigns each day.

34. "Real Eyes"

With eyes that see, and a heart that knows,
We navigate the world through its ebbs and flows.
But amidst the truth and the lies we're told,
It's hard to discern what's real and what's cold.

Real eyes realise real lies,
Behind the masks and the disguised guise.
They see the intentions and the hidden agendas too,
And distinguish truth from the false and the new.

With real eyes, we see the world anew,
Unveiling the deceptions and the lies that shine through.
We're not deceived by the facade and the show,
For real eyes realise the truth that others may not know.

So let us keep our eyes open wide,
And see the world with a discerning stride.
For real eyes realise real lies,
And guide us through with a heart that's wise.

In a world of illusions and deceptive sights,
Real eyes are the gifts that shine with inner light.
They illuminate the path and show us the way,
To navigate life's challenges, come what may.

So cherish your real eyes and the truth they reveal,
For they are the guardians of your heart and your zeal.
And when the world outside is shrouded in disguise,
Your real eyes will guide you to the truth that never dies.

Through the noise and the chaos, they will lead the way,
And help you find your footing on a brand new day.
With real eyes, you'll see the world with clarity,
And make decisions that align with your heart's
sincerity.

So let us cultivate these real eyes of ours,
And use them to navigate life's joys and its scars.
For with real eyes, we'll see the truth in all its forms,
And live a life that's authentic and free from life's storms.

In a world that's full of deception and hidden agendas
too,
Real eyes are the keys that unlock the truth anew.
So let us keep them open and use them every day,
To see the world with clarity and find our way.

35. "The Beauty of Self love "

My goal is to give myself everything I deserve,
To shower my soul with love and let my heart swerve.
From the chains of self-doubt and the weights of fear,
I'll rise up and let my true self appear.

I'll give myself kindness, compassion, and care,
And wrap my arms around myself with love to share.
I'll celebrate my strengths and acknowledge my flaws,
And treat myself with gentle hands and a loving pause.

I'll listen to my intuition and trust my inner voice,
And make choices that align with my heart's joyful
choice.
I'll take time to nourish my body and soothe my mind,
And prioritize my well-being, leaving stress and worry
behind.

I'll be my own best friend and stand by my side,
Through life's ups and downs, and every step of the ride.
I'll give myself forgiveness and let go of the past,

And welcome each new moment with an open heart that
will last.

My goal is to give myself everything I deserve,
To live a life that's authentic and filled with love that
serves.
So I'll keep on shining and let my light be bright,
And give myself the gift of self-love every single night.

With every breath, I'll choose to love myself more,
And honor my worth with a heart that's pure and whole.
I'll let go of perfection and embrace my unique soul,
And celebrate my individuality with a heart that's free.

I'll trust my own wisdom and listen to my heart,
And make decisions that align with my deepest part.
I'll be gentle with myself and kind to my own skin,
And treat myself with the love that I'd offer to a friend
within.

So here's to self-love and the gift it brings to me,
A life of authenticity and a heart that's wild and free.
May I continue to shine and let my light be bright,
And give myself the gift of self-love every single night.

36. "A Life of Purpose"

Be a good person, with a heart so true,
Don't waste your time trying to prove it to a few.
Let your actions speak louder than your words,
And let your kindness shine like a beacon that's heard.

Don't seek validation from those who can't see,
The beauty of your soul and the goodness in you.
For true character is shown in the deeds that you do,
Not in the opinions of others, who may not be true.

Be a good person because it's who you are,
Not to impress others or to reach some distant star.
Let your integrity guide you like a compass in the night,
And let your heart shine bright, with all its light.

So don't waste your time trying to prove your worth,
Just be a good person, and let your actions give birth
To a life of purpose, and a heart that's free,
A life that's authentic, and a soul that's meant to be.

For in the end, it's not what others think,
That matters most, but the goodness that you link
To your heart, your soul, and every deed,
That's what makes you a good person, indeed.

37. "Detours and Destinations"

Life's journey is full of twists and turns,
Detours and delays that our souls yearn.
We board the wrong train, with a sigh of dismay,
Only to find ourselves at the right station someday.

Nothing is good or bad; it's just a test,
A chance to grow, learn, and find our best.
The wrong path leads us to the right place,
Where we discover strengths and a wiser face.

We question fate and the universe's plan,
But sometimes the wrong train takes us to the promised
land.
So we trust the journey and let go of fear,
And find that detours lead us to our deepest cheer.

For in the end, it's not the route we take,
But the wisdom we gain and the love we make.
The wrong train becomes the right one in time,

And we arrive at our destination with a heart that's
aligned.

So let's not worry about twists and turns,
But trust that life's journey will take us to our concerns.
For sometimes the wrong train takes us to the right
station,
And we find ourselves exactly where we need to be, in
perfect formation.

And when we look back on the journey we've made,
We'll see that detours were stepping stones we've laid.
For every wrong turn led us to a new view,
And every delay gave us time to renew.

So let's trust the journey and let go of our fears,
And know that every step leads us to our deepest cheers.
For life's journey is full of twists, turns, and bends,
But with trust and faith, we'll find our way to our truest
friends.

And when we finally arrive at our destination so grand,
We'll look back on the journey and see the beauty of the
land.
For every detour, delay, wrong turn, and bend
Led us to where we are and helped us transcend.

38. "Value Your Time"

Be selfish with your time; it's a precious thing,
Don't waste it on those who don't make your heart sing.
A lot of people don't deserve a minute of your day,
So guard your time and only give it away.

To those who uplift and support you on your way,
To those who bring joy and laughter to brighten your
day.
But to those who drain your energy and bring you pain,
Be selfish and keep your distance; don't give them your
time in vain.

Your time is valuable; it's a gift to yourself,
Don't squander it on those who don't deserve your
wealth.
Invest it in yourself, in your passions, and your dreams,
And only share it with those who help your heart beam.

So be selfish with your time; it's okay to say no,

*To those who don't deserve it and to things that don't
make you glow.
You deserve to spend your time on what sets your soul
on fire,
So guard your time and only share it with those who
inspire.*

*Don't let others dictate how you spend your time,
Take control of your schedule and make it truly yours.
Learn to say no without feeling guilty or ashamed,
Remember, your time is precious, and it's not to be
claimed.*

*By others who don't respect your boundaries and space,
Who don't value your time and don't know its true pace.
So guard your time like a treasure rare,
And only share it with those who show they truly care.*

*For time is a gift that we can't get back,
So let's use it wisely and never look back.
On moments wasted, on hours that slipped away,
But instead, let's focus on living each day.*

*To the fullest, with purpose and with zest,
With time well spent, and a heart that's at rest.
So guard your time and use it with care,
And remember, it's yours, and yours alone to share.*

39. "The Peace of Anonymity"

In the shadows, I find my peace,
A world away from prying eyes' release.
No judgments made, no expectations high,
Just the freedom to live, without a sigh.

Life is better when nobody knows my name,
When strangers pass, without a hint of fame.
No whispers spread, no rumors take flight,
Just the quiet comfort of a peaceful night.

In anonymity, I find my strength,
A shield from criticism, a refuge from length.
No comparisons made, no competitions won,
Just the simple joy of living, one by one.

The world may think me invisible, unknown,
But in my solitude, I am finally home.
No masks to wear, no roles to play,
Just the pure delight of living life my way.

So let me bask in the beauty of being unseen,
And find my happiness in the quiet, peaceful scene.
For in the stillness, I discover my voice,
And in anonymity, I find my heart's rejoice.

In this quiet space, I find my truth,
A place where I can be myself, without pretense or
youth.
No apologies given, no explanations made,
Just the freedom to live, without a hint of shame.

So let me cherish this anonymity,
This gift of silence, this peaceful serenity.
For in its depths, I find my soul's retreat,
A place where I can heal, and find my heart's beat.

In this stillness, I find my creative spark,
A flame that flickers bright, without a single mark.
No criticism made, no judgments passed,
Just the pure joy of creating, without a single glass.

So let me bask in this anonymity's bliss,
And find my happiness in the quiet, peaceful kiss.
For in its depths, I find my heart's delight,
A place where I can shine, without a single fight.

40. "Kindness Makes You Rare"

In a world that's often loud and gray,
Kindness is a color that brightens up the day.
It's a gentle touch, a listening ear,
A compassionate heart that wipes away the tear.

Kindness is a gift that's rare and true,
A treasure that's precious and shines right through.
It's a bridge that connects, a bond that ties,
A love that's unconditional and never dies.

In a sea of faces, kindness makes you stand,
A beacon of hope in a world so grand.
It's a whisper of warmth on a cold and lonely night,
A guiding light that shines and leads to what's right.

So let kindness be your compass, your guiding star,
Your North, your South, your near and far.
For kindness makes you rare, a gem so bright,
A treasure to behold in the dark of night.

In a world that's often harsh and cold,
Kindness is a flame that never grows old.
It's a love that's pure, a heart that's true,
A kindness that's rare and shines right through.

41. "The Struggle is Strength"

The weight you carry, the burden you bear,
Is shaping your shoulders, and preparing you to share
The load of tomorrow, the trials yet to come,
Will require the strength you're building, one struggle at
a time, one step at a time, one breath at a time.

The fire you're walking through, the flames that seem so
high,
Are refining your spirit, and purifying your heart's cry.
The heat of the moment, the pressure that's applied,
Is tempering your will, and strengthening your stride.

The darkness you're facing, the shadows that loom near,
Are teaching you to trust, and to hold on to hope and
fear.
The uncertainty of it all, the unknown that lies ahead,
Is developing your faith, and strengthening your heart's
thread.

So don't be discouraged, don't lose your way,
For the struggle you're in today is developing the
strength you need for tomorrow's day.
It's building your resilience, your courage, and your
might,
And preparing you for the victories that will soon shine
with new light.

Remember, every step you take, every breath you make,
Is a testament to your strength and your will to partake
In the journey that's unfolding, with every trial and test,
You're becoming stronger, more resilient, and more
blessed.

The struggles you're facing, the challenges you're
overcoming,
Are the catalysts for growth and the building blocks of
your becoming.
So don't be afraid to face them, to walk through the fire,
For on the other side, you'll find your greatest desire.

A stronger, wiser, more compassionate you,
A person who's been tempered, refined, and renewed.
A person who's been tested, tried, and proven true,
A person who's emerging, stronger, brighter, and anew.

42. "Embracing the Storm"

Life's journey is not a gentle breeze,
But a raging storm that tests your ease.
It's a path fraught with trials and strife,
A road paved with challenges, and a future rife.

With uncertainty and doubt, you'll face the test,
And times when fear and worry will be your constant
guests.
But in the midst of turmoil, don't lose your way,
For it's in the darkness that you'll find the strength to
stay.

Accept the reality that life won't be easy,
That every step forward will require courage and
tenacity.
You'll need to dig deep to find the will to carry on,
To push through the pain and rise above the dawn.

But in the fire of adversity, you'll be refined,
Your spirit strengthened, your heart aligned.

You'll learn to bend, not break, to flex, not fold,
To rise above the noise and find your inner gold.

So don't be fooled by the calm, the peaceful shore,
For life's journey is a stormy sea, and you'll need to
navigate more.
But with every wave, every gust of wind,
You'll find the strength to carry on, rise above, and begin.

To begin anew, start again, find the courage to face
The challenges ahead, the unknown, the uncertain pace.
So accept the reality that life won't be easy,
But know you're strong, and you'll rise above the sea.

43. "Don't Let Them Bring You Down"

There are people who will try to bring you pain,
To ruin your day and drive you insane.
They'll speak their minds with words so unkind,
And try to bring you down with their toxic mind.

But don't let them win, don't let them succeed
In ruining your day and planting a seed
Of doubt and fear, of anger and stress,
In your mind and heart, where love and joy should rest.

You are stronger than their words, their opinions, their
hate.
You are a shining star that can't be diminished or late.
Your worth and value come from within, not from
without,
So don't let the idiots bring you down or make you
doubt.

Rise above their noise, their negativity, their pain,

And find your inner peace, your joy, your love, your
gain.
Surround yourself with people who uplift and inspire,
And don't let the idiots ruin your day or set your soul on
fire.

Remember, you are loved, you are valued, you are strong,
And don't let anyone make you feel otherwise, all day
long.
So hold your head high, keep your heart light,
And don't let the idiots ruin your day or your life.

You are a warrior, a survivor, a soul so bright,
Don't let the haters bring you down without a fight.
You've got this; you're strong, capable, and brave,
Don't let anyone make you feel otherwise; you're a rock,
a wave.

So rise up, take a stand, and show them your might,
Don't let the idiots bring you down without a fight.
You are a shining star that shines bright and bold,
Don't let anyone dim your light; you're a treasure to
behold.

Keep shining, keep sparkling, keep rising above,
Don't let the idiots bring you down with their toxic love.
You are loved, valued, strong, and bright,

*Don't let anyone make you feel otherwise; you're a
precious light.*

44. "Fearless and Free"

She stands tall, with a heart so bold,
A warrior spirit that never grows old.
She faces challenges with a fierce cry,
And rises above with a determined sigh.

Her soul is unbreakable, her will unshaken,
She walks through the fire with her head held high,
unspoken.
She is a force of nature, a stormy sea,
Unstoppable and fierce, wild and carefree.

She is a phoenix rising from the ashes born,
A shining star that lights up the morn.
She is a lioness with a heart so bright,
A beacon of hope in the dark of night.

She is strong, she is brave, she is fearless too,
A true warrior with a spirit anew.
She is a survivor, a thriver, a soul so bright,
She is a woman with a heart full of light.

*She has been through the storm and emerged stronger
still,*
Her roots run deep, her spirit unbroken and fulfilled.
She has faced her fears and overcome her doubts,
And risen above with a heart that shouts.

So let her roar, let her soar, let her be,
A symbol of strength for you and me.
For she is strong, she is brave, she is free,
A true inspiration for all humanity.

She is a reminder that we all have the power
To rise above and shine in each hour.
She is a testament to the strength of the soul,
A shining example of what it means to be whole.

So let us celebrate this strong and brave woman,
Who inspires us all to be our best version.
Let us honor her strength and her courageous heart,
And let us strive to be as strong and brave from the start.

45. "Silent Strength"

I may be quiet, but don't think me weak,
My silence is strength, my heart speaks.
I observe and listen, I absorb and learn,
My quiet nature is not a sign of concern.

My words are chosen wisely, each one a deliberate
thought,
I speak with intention, my voice is not caught.
In the stillness, I find my power and might,
My quiet strength is a force that shines so bright.

I am not one for noise, drama, or fray,
But when I speak, my words have weight and sway.
I am a thinker, a feeler, a soul so deep,
My quiet nature is just a part of who I keep.

I see the world from a unique view,
A perspective that's true.
I hear the whispers of the heart,
A language that's unspoken, yet never departs.

So don't mistake my silence for weakness or fear,
For in the quiet, I find my strength and cheer.
I may be quiet, but I am not weak,
My silent strength is a power that I uniquely speak.

I'll use my voice when the time is right,
To speak my truth and shine with all my light.
I'll stand tall and proud, with a heart so bold,
My silent strength will be the foundation that never
grows old.

I'll be the calm in the storm, the peace in the night,
A beacon of hope, shining with all my might.
I'll be the quiet one, with a heart so bright,
My silent strength will be the guiding light.

46. "Victory's Price"

No triumph comes without a test,
No victory won without a quest.
For every gain, a cost is paid,
A sacrifice made, a price displayed.

The path to success is rarely easy,
It winds and turns, with obstacles breezy.
It demands of us our time, our sweat, our tears,
And sometimes, it requires us to face our deepest fears.

But it's in these moments of trial and strife,
That we discover our inner strength and life.
For every sacrifice we make, we grow,
And with each challenge, our spirit glows.

So let us not be deterred by the cost,
But instead, let us be willing to pay the price we've lost.
For in the end, it's not the sacrifice that we make,
But the victory we win, that our hearts will undertake.

No victory comes without a fight,
No triumph won without a sacrifice in sight.
But it's in the struggle, that we find our might,
And in the victory, our hearts take flight.

Through the fire and the rain, we'll find our way,
And emerge stronger, come what may.
For every sacrifice, a reward is gained,
And in the victory, our hearts are sustained.

So let us rise to the challenge, and make our stand,
With courage and strength, we'll take our rightful land.
For we are warriors, with hearts untamed,
And our victory will be the prize we've claimed.

47. "Rare Connection"

I don't connect with just anyone,
My energy's selective, my vibes are done.
I don't force it, I don't pretend,
My relationships are genuine, or they end.

I'd rather be alone, with my thoughts astray,
Than fake a connection, day by day.
I need depth, I need substance, I need fire,
Or I'll just fade away, like a dying desire.

But when I do connect, it's real and true,
A bond forms strong, a friendship shines through.
We vibe on the same wave, our hearts beat as one,
In a world of noise, our connection is won.

It's rare, but it's real, this connection we share,
A bond that's unbreakable, a friendship that's rare.
We don't need words, we don't need space,
Our connection's pure, our vibe's in place.

So I'll wait for the ones who resonate with me,
Who share my energy, my frequency.
I'll wait for the connections that are real and true,
For with them, my heart beats anew.

Through the chaos, I'll find my way,
To those who see me, day by day.
I'll recognize them by the vibe they give,
A sense of home, a sense of living.

In their presence, I'll feel alive,
A spark will ignite, a fire will thrive.
Our connection will grow, flourish, and bloom,
A rare and beautiful thing, a treasure to assume.

48. "The Measure of a Man"

A man's true character is not revealed by fame,
Nor by the wealth that he may gain.
It's not by the power that he may hold,
But by the way he treats those who are old.

It's not by the words that he may say,
But by the actions that he takes each day.
It's by the way he treats the poor and the weak,
And those who can do nothing for him to seek.

A man's character is revealed by his heart,
By the way he treats those who are torn apart.
It's by the kindness that he shows to those in need,
And by the compassion that he gives with speed.

So let us not be fooled by outward show,
But let us look to the heart that beats below.
For it's there that we will find the measure of a man,
And the true character that he has in his plan.

It's in the way he treats the stranger in his land,
The way he welcomes those who are lost and grand.
It's in the way he listens to the stories untold,
And the way he helps those who are young and old.

It's in the way he stands up for what is right,
And the way he fights for justice with all his might.
It's in the way he shows compassion and empathy too,
And the way he treats all people with kindness and truth.

So let us look to the heart of a man,
And not be fooled by the outward plan.
For it's there that we will find the true measure of a man,
And the character that he has, and the plan that he can

49. "Rise Again"

You can fall, but you can't stay down,
For every setback, there's a comeback town.
It's a place where mindset is the key,
Where resilience blooms, and hope sets free.

You can lose, but you can't lose your way,
For every failure, there's a new day.
It's a chance to rise, to stand tall and strong,
To turn your weaknesses into a brand new song.

You can face your fears, and overcome your doubts,
For every obstacle, there's a way to shout.
It's a voice that whispers, "You are enough",
A voice that echoes, "You can rise above".

It's all about mindset, the way you think and see,
The way you approach life, with positivity and glee.
You can comeback from anything, no matter the test,
With a mindset that's strong, and a heart that's blessed.

So don't give up, don't lose your faith,
For every comeback, there's a new escape.
Rise again, rise strong, rise free,
With a mindset that's unstoppable, wild, and carefree.

Through the darkness, you'll find a way
To rise above the pain and seize the day.
You'll learn to bend, but never break,
And find a way to make your spirit awake.

You'll rise above the noise and the pain,
And find a voice that speaks your truth again.
You'll stand together, and support each other's might,
And shine your light in the darkest of nights.

So let us march on this journey we call life,
With a mindset that's strong and a heart that's rife.
We'll face our fears, and overcome our doubts,
And emerge victorious, with our spirits devout.

We'll rise again, we'll rise strong,
We'll rise free, with a heart that's not wrong.
We'll shine our light in the darkest of nights,
And guide each other through life's plights.

50. "Words Have Power"

Be careful with your words, they have might,
They can lift up or tear down in a fight.
You never know how many times they'll replay,
In someone's head, long after you've gone away.

A careless phrase, a thoughtless remark,
Can echo on, leaving a lasting mark.
It can haunt and hurt, or heal and mend,
The power of words, a true and lasting trend.

So choose your words with care and kindness too,
For you never know what someone's going through.
A gentle phrase, a supportive line,
Can be a lifeline, a beacon that shines.

But harsh words, they can cut like a knife,
Leaving scars that may never heal in life.
So let's be mindful of the words we say,
For they have power, and can make or break a day.

Let's use our words to uplift and inspire,
To bring hope and joy, and set hearts on fire.
For words have power, and can change a life,
So let's choose them wisely, and use them to thrive.

Let's think before we speak, and consider the weight,
Of the words we choose, and the impact they create.
Let's use our words to build, to heal, and to mend,
And not to tear down, or to offend.

For words have power, and can be a blessing or a curse,
So let's choose them wisely, and use them to traverse
The path of kindness, compassion, and love,
And to make a positive impact, sent from above.

51. "A Life of Freedom"

In life's grand tapestry, we're threads of might,
Yearning to break free from endless night.
Freedom's the goal, the beacon that shines bright,
The only worthy aim, the guiding light.

But how do we attain this treasured state?
By letting go of things that fate can't wait.
The whims of others, the twists of chance,
The things that lie beyond our mortal dance.

We must disregard the noise, the constant din,
The opinions, expectations, and the judgments within.
We must focus on the things that we can control,
Our thoughts, our actions, our hearts, our soul.

For freedom's not a gift that's handed down,
But a choice we make, a path we wear down.
It's the decision to let go of the reins,
To break free from the chains that bind and restrain.

So let us walk this path, with hearts untamed,
And minds that soar, unencumbered by the games.
Let us disregard the things that we can't command,
And focus on the freedom that's ours to expand.

Let us not be held back by the fears of others,
Nor be swayed by the opinions of those who would
smother.
Let us rise above the noise, and shine our light,
And let our freedom be the guiding force of our might.

For freedom is the fire that burns within our soul,
A flame that flickers bright, and makes our hearts whole.
It's the wind that lifts our wings, and sets us free,
A gift that's ours to claim, and one that's meant to be.

So let us claim our freedom, and let it be our guide,
And let us walk the path, that's ours to abide.
For freedom is the only worthy goal in life,
And it's won by disregarding things that lie beyond our
strife.

52. "Strength with Heart"

Be strong, but not rude; be brave, but not bold,
For kindness and compassion never grow old.
Stand up for what's right, but do it with a gentle hand,
For strength and love can go together, across this land.

Don't let your words cut deep or your actions cause pain,
For being strong doesn't mean you have to be harsh or
vain.
Instead, let your heart guide you, and let your words be
kind and true,
For that's where true strength lies, in being strong and
gentle too.

Be a rock for those who need you, a shelter from life's
storm,
But don't let your strength turn to stone, or your heart
become a form.
Keep your heart open and soft, and your spirit free and
bright,

*For that's where your true strength lies, in being strong
and shining light.*

*So be strong, but not rude; be brave, but not bold,
For kindness and compassion never grow old.
Stand up for what's right, but do it with a gentle hand,
For strength and love can go together, across this land.*

*Let your strength be a beacon that shines for all to see,
A guiding light that leads the way to a brighter destiny.
Let your heart be a sanctuary where love and kindness
reign,
A safe haven where others can find refuge and feel no
pain.*

*For true strength is not about being tough or hard as
stone,
But about being gentle, compassionate, and kind, and
making a positive tone.
It's about standing up for what's right, but doing it with
a gentle hand,
And being a rock for those who need you, while keeping
your heart open and grand.*

53. "Forged in Fire"

Pain is the fire that burns within,
A flame that flickers, yet never gives in.
It's the weight that's lifted, the trial that's faced,
The darkness that's navigated, the storm that's placed.

Comfort is the calm that soothes the soul,
A gentle breeze that whispers, "You're in control."
But comfort can be a curse, a crutch that's leaned on,
A weakness that's cultivated, a strength that's
overthrown.

Pain builds you, it breaks you, it molds you, it makes
A stronger, wiser, more resilient heart that beats.
It's the fire that forges, the hammer that shapes,
The trials that temper, the struggles that create.

Comfort weakens you, it softens, it soothes, it calms,
But it also stagnates, suffocates, and disarms.
It's the calm before the storm, the silence before the
scream,

*The stillness before the chaos, the quiet before the
extreme.*

*So let the fire burn, let the pain shape and mold,
For it's in the darkness that we find our greatest gold.
Let the struggles strengthen, let the trials refine,
For it's in the fire that we're forged, and our true selves
align.*

*Let the flames of adversity purify your soul,
And let the heat of the fire transform you, making you
whole.
For in the fire, you'll find the strength to carry on,
And in the pain, you'll discover the resilience to be
reborn.*

*Don't be afraid to walk through the fire,
For it's in the flames that you'll find your heart's desire.
Don't be afraid to face the pain,
For it's in the struggle that you'll find your greatest gain.*

54. "The Art of Victory"

In the realm of war, where strength is key,
A subtle strategy can set the enemy free.
The supreme art of war, a paradox to some,
Is to subdue the enemy without a single drum.

It's not about brute force or violence and might,
But about outsmarting, outmaneuvering, and staying out
of sight.
A clever tactic and a strategic mind
Can conquer the foe without a single wound to find.

Sun Tzu's wisdom, a timeless guide,
Teaches us to avoid strength and attack the enemy's
pride.
To disrupt their plans, sow discord and fear,
And emerge victorious without a single spear.

The art of victory, subtle and refined,
Involves patience, persistence, and a deep design.
It's not about winning battles but winning the war,

By subduing the enemy without a single roar.

*So let us learn from the masters, from Sun Tzu's ancient
text,*
*The art of war, subtle and complex, yet simple and
correct.*
For in the end, it's not about fighting and bloodshed,
*But about emerging victorious with minimal cost and
dread.*

Let us adapt, evolve, and outmaneuver,
For in the art of war, flexibility is the key to deliver.
Let us use our minds and wit
*To outsmart the enemy and emerge victorious without a
single hit.*

*For the true art of war is not about destruction and
chaos,*
*But about creation, order, and bringing peace to the
masses.*
*It's about using our strength not to dominate and
oppress,*
But to protect, serve, and bring freedom and happiness.

So let us master the art of war, learn from the past,
*And use our knowledge to create a brighter future that
will forever last.*

55. "A Moment's Choice"

The future beckons, uncertain and wide,
A path unwinding, where choices will reside.
The present moment, a crossroads we stand,
Where decisions made, will shape the future's hand.

What we do today, will mold tomorrow's fate,
A single choice, can alter the course we create.
The future's canvas, a blank and waiting space,
Where every brushstroke, of our present, will leave its
mark and place.

We hold the power, to shape what's yet to be,
To craft a future, where hope and dreams can be free.
But we must act, with intention and with care,
For the choices we make, will determine the future we'll
share.

So let us choose, with wisdom and with heart,
To create a future, where love and kindness will never
depart.

Let us tend the garden, of our present with care,
And nurture the seeds, of a brighter future we'll share.

For the future depends, on what we do today,
On the choices we make, and the path we'll sway.
So let us walk, with purpose and with might,
And shape the future, with the light of our present sight.

Let us not wait, for tomorrow's uncertain dawn,
But seize the moment, and make our choices born.
For in the present, we hold the power to create,
A future that's bright, and a destiny that's great.

So let us choose, to live with intention and care,
To make each moment, a step towards a brighter future
we'll share.
Let us tend the flame, of our inner light,
And guide ourselves, through the darkness of night.

For the future is ours, to shape and to mold,
To create a world, where love and kindness unfold.
So let us walk, with purpose and with heart,
And shape the future, with the light of our present start.

56. "Worthy of Love"

I deserve to be loved, to be cherished and adored,
To be treated with kindness, and respected to the core.
I deserve to be heard, to have my voice be clear,
To be seen and understood, without fear.

I deserve to be happy, to live a life that's true,
To pursue my passions, and make my dreams come
through.
I deserve to be free, to make my own choices and
decisions,
To live a life that's authentic, without conditions.

I deserve to be surrounded by people who uplift and
inspire,
Who support me and encourage me to reach for my
highest desire.
I deserve to be loved without condition or shame,
To be accepted for who I am, without needing to change.

I deserve to take care of my body, mind, and soul,

To nurture and nourish myself, and make myself whole.
I deserve to be gentle with myself and others too,
To practice self-love and self-care, and see it through.

I deserve to shine, to let my light be seen,
To share my gifts and talents, and make a positive impact
on the scene.
I deserve to be proud of who I am and what I've done,
To celebrate my successes, and have fun.

57. "The Language of Kindness"

Kindness is a language that transcends the senses,
A dialect that's understood by all, in every essence.
It's a tongue that's spoken without words or sound,
A gentle whisper that echoes all around.

The blind can see it in the touch of a hand,
A guiding light that leads them through uncertain lands.
The deaf can hear it in the vibrations of the heart,
A rhythm that beats with compassion and never departs.

It's a language that's universal and knows no bounds,
A bridge that connects us all without a single sound.
It's a dialect spoken by the soul,
A gentle murmur that makes us whole.

With every act of kindness, we speak this language true,
A tongue understood by all in all we do.
So let us speak it loudly with every deed and every word,
And fill the world with kindness like a love unheard.

Let us speak it in silence when words are hard to find,
Let us speak it in noise when chaos surrounds.
Let us speak it with our actions with every step and
every stride,
Let us speak it with our hearts and let kindness be our
guide.

For kindness is a language understood by all,
A universal dialect transcending every wall.
It's a language that heals, mends, and restores,
A language bringing us together forevermore.

58. "Resilience"

Life's journey is not a gentle breeze,
But a raging storm that tests our ease.
It's a path that's fraught with twists and turns,
A road that's paved with trials and concerns.

We must accept the reality that life won't be easy,
That every step forward will be met with resistance and
unease.
But it's in these moments that we discover our strength,
A resilience that's born from the depths of our being.

We must be brave and face our fears,
And stand tall through all our tears.
We must be strong and hold on tight,
And never give up without a fight.

For life is precious, and every moment counts,
And though it may be hard, we must never doubt
Our ability to rise above the pain and strife,
And find a way to thrive in life.

So let us stand and face the test,
And show the world that we are blessed.
With a strength that's deep and a spirit that's bright,
We'll shine like stars in the dark of night.

Through the darkness, we'll find our way,
And emerge stronger with each new day.
We'll learn to bend but never break,
And find a way to make our spirits awake.

We'll rise above the noise and the pain,
And find a voice that speaks our truth again.
We'll stand together and support each other's might,
And shine our light in the darkest of nights.

So let us march on this journey we call life,
With resilience and strength as our guiding light.
We'll face our fears and overcome our doubts,
And emerge victorious with our spirits devout.

59. "Seize the Moment"

We wait and wait for the perfect time,
For the stars to align and the moment to shine.
But as we wait, life slips away,
And opportunities lost leave us with nothing to say.

The right time is now, not tomorrow or next year,
For procrastination is a thief that steals our hopes and
fear.
It whispers sweet nothings of a better day ahead,
But as we wait, our dreams and goals are left for dead.

The perfect moment is a myth, a fantasy,
For the only moment that truly exists is now, in reality.
So let us seize it with both hands and heart,
And make the most of it before it falls apart.

For waiting for the right time is just another way
Of wasting time and letting life slip away.
So let us act now with courage and might,

And make our dreams a reality in the light of day and
night.

Let us not wait for the perfect circumstance,
For the perfect moment is a fleeting glance.
Let us take the leap with faith and trust,
And make the most of the moment that we have been
given, just.

For time is a river that flows swiftly by,
And if we wait too long, we'll miss the tide.
So let us seize the moment with both hands and heart,
And make the most of it before we depart.

Let us not let fear hold us back from our dreams,
For the greatest risk is not taking the leap, it seems.
Let us be brave and take the first step,
And make our dreams a reality with every breath we
take and every step.

60. "From Growth to Glory"

In realms of self, where growth is key,
True nobility lies in being more than we used to be.
It's not in titles, wealth, or fame,
But in the progress we make and the person we reclaim.

The past is past, with all its flaws and fears,
But we can rise above and wipe away our tears.
For every step forward is a step away
From the person we were and the mistakes we'd make
each day.

True nobility lies in self-improvement's might,
In being superior to our former self's plight.
It's in the lessons learned and the wisdom we gain,
In the strength we build and the love we sustain.

So let us strive to be more than we were,
To rise above and show the world we care.
For true nobility is not in what we own,

But in the person we become and the progress we've
known.

Let us celebrate our growth and our might,
And honor the journey that's led us to this light.
For every step forward is a step away
From the person we were and the mistakes we'd make
each day.

Let us not be held back by the chains of our past,
But let us rise above and forge a new path at last.
Let us learn from our mistakes and use them as a guide,
And let us strive to be better with each passing tide.

For true nobility is not a destination, but a journey,
A path of self-discovery and continuous growth and
learning.
So let us embark on this journey with courage and heart,
And let us rise above to a new and better start.

61. "A Warrior's Heart"

In the depths of our soul, a fire burns bright,
A flame of resilience that guides us through the night.
It's a strength we never knew we possessed within,
Until the trials of life forced us to dig deep and begin.

We thought we were weak, fragile, and frail,
But the weight of our burdens revealed a strength that
never failed.
It's a strength forged in fire and tempered in pain,
A strength born of necessity and the will to rise above
the strain.

You never know how strong you are until being strong is
your only choice,
Until the darkness closes in, and you're forced to make a
voice.
It's a voice that's loud and clear, strong and free,
A voice that echoes through the night and shines like a
beacon in the sea.

So don't be fooled by your fears or the doubts that creep
into your mind,
For you are stronger than you think, and your spirit is
hard to unwind.
You've survived every stormy night and every dark and
troubled day,
And you've emerged stronger, wiser, and more resilient
in every way.

So hold your head up high and let your spirit soar,
For you are a warrior, a fighter, and a survivor,
forevermore.
You've got a strength within you waiting to be
unleashed,
A strength unique to you and a power yet to be seized.

Let the fire of your soul burn brighter with each passing
day,
And let the strength of your spirit guide you through
life's uncertain way.
For you are capable of greatness, and your potential is
yet to be told,
So rise up and let your strength shine like a beacon in
the cold.

Don't let the shadows of doubt creep in and steal your
light,

For you are a shining star burning bright in the night.
You've got a strength within you waiting to be set free,
A strength unique to you and a power yet to be.

So let your spirit soar, and let your heart be brave,
For you are a warrior, a fighter, and a survivor in every
way.
You've got a strength within you waiting to be
unleashed,
A strength unique to you and a power yet to be seized.

62. "A Path of Courage"

Take a moment to breathe and reflect on your way,
Think of the struggles, the trials, and the darkest of days.
You've walked through the fire and emerged from the
night,
Stronger, wiser, and braver, with a heart that's still
bright.

So thank yourself for the journey, for the strength you've
gained,
For the lessons you've learned, and the love you've
sustained.
It hasn't been easy; there have been times you've felt
worn,
But you've picked yourself up and kept moving forward,
reborn.

You've faced your fears and overcome your doubts,
You've found a resilience within that's carried you
through life's routs.
You've discovered a strength you never knew you had,

A strength forged in fire and tempered like steel, not bad.

So be proud of yourself for how far you've come,
For the battles you've fought and the wars you've won.
You've earned the right to celebrate, to honor your name,
You've earned the right to thank yourself for the strength
you've gained.

It's okay to look back, to remember the pain,
But don't get stuck in the past; keep moving forward,
maintain.
The journey ahead is still uncertain and long,
But you've got the strength to keep moving, to keep
going strong.

So thank yourself for the journey so far,
For the strength you've gained and the scars that you've
marred.
You're stronger than you think, braver than you feel,
So keep moving forward and never forget to heal.

Remember the moments that made you feel alive,
The moments that tested you and made you thrive.
Remember the people who helped you along the way,
And the lessons you've learned that have made you
stronger each day.

So hold your head up high and let your spirit soar,
You've got a strength within you that you've never
known before.
You've got a resilience that's carried you through the
night,
And a heart that's still beating, with a fire that's still
bright.

Keep moving forward and never give up the fight,
You're stronger than you think, and you're shining with
all your might.
So thank yourself for the journey so far,
And know that you've got the strength to go even
farther.

63. "Authentic Self"

In the depths of your journey, through trials and strife,
You lost sight of yourself and your inner light.
But now you've found your way back to your heart's
core,
And rediscovered the you that you'd been searching for.

Don't let yourself go now that you're found;
Hold on to your essence and keep your spirit sound.
You've worked hard to reclaim your authenticity and
might,
Don't let the world outside dull your shine so bright.

Remember the struggles that made you stronger and
wise,
And the lessons you've learned that opened your eyes.
You've grown, you've evolved, and you've become more
you,
Don't let anyone or anything take that away from you.

When the world tries to mold and shape you to its will,

Resist the pressure and stay true to your inner still.
Don't compromise your values or sacrifice your soul;
You're worth more than that, and your worth makes you
whole.

So hold on to yourself and never let go;
You're a unique and precious gem that shines like a glow.
Keep your light burning bright and your heart beating
strong,
You've found yourself again, and now you can't go
wrong.

Don't let the noise of the world drown out your inner
voice;
Stay true to yourself and make your own choice.
You've got the power to create the life you want to lead,
So hold on to your dreams and never let them bleed.

Remember the moments that made you feel alive,
The moments that tested you and made you thrive.
You've got the strength within to overcome any test,
So hold on to yourself and always do your best.

So keep shining your light and never let it fade;
You're a beacon of hope in a world that's often afraid.
You've found yourself again, and now you're free to be
The best version of yourself, wild and carefree.

64. "The Fight Within"

If you're still breathing, then your fight's not done,
Your story's still unfolding, your journey's just begun.
The struggles you've faced, the trials you've borne,
Have strengthened your spirit and prepared you for
more.

Don't give up the fight, don't lose your way;
Your voice still matters, your life still has sway.
Every breath you take is a chance to start anew,
To rise up and keep fighting for all that you hold true.

Your scars are a testament to the battles you've won,
Your heart still beats strong, your spirit has just begun.
To falter, to fail, is not the end of the fight;
It's just a setback, a chance to rise up and shine with all
your might.

So don't lose faith, don't lose hope;
Your fight is far from over, your story still unfolds.
Keep pushing forward, keep striving to be

The best version of yourself, wild and carefree.

Remember the fire that burns deep within your soul,
The passion that drives you to reach your highest goal.
Don't let the flames of doubt extinguish your light;
Keep pushing forward through the dark of night.

You've survived every storm that's come your way,
You've risen above the pain and found a brighter day.
So don't give up now, don't lose your stride;
Keep moving forward with your heart as your guide.

If you're still breathing, then your fight's not done,
Your life still has purpose, your journey's just begun.
So rise up, take a breath, and let your spirit soar;
Your unfinished battle is still worth fighting for.

Don't let the world outside dictate your fate;
You have the power to choose your own path to create.
So keep pushing forward through the ups and downs,
And always remember, your strength wears the crown.

65. "From Ashes to Glory"

Your past may be marked by scars and pain,
But that doesn't define the life you'll gain.
The wounds that once seemed impossible to heal,
Can become the strength that helps you reveal.

The darkness you faced, the struggles you bore,
Can be the catalyst for a brighter tomorrow.
The lessons you learned, the wisdom you gained,
Can guide you towards a future that's not stained.

You are not your past, you are not your shame,
You are the sum of your choices, and your future's to
claim.
You can rise above the ashes, like a phoenix born,
And create a life that's filled with hope, love, and morn.

Don't let your history define your destiny,
You have the power to create a new reality.
Take the lessons from your past, and use them to thrive,
And create a future that's brighter, and more alive.

You are stronger than you think, braver than you feel,
And capable of achieving greatness, and making your
dreams real.
So don't give up, don't lose hope,
Keep pushing forward, and never look back.

Your future is waiting, like a blank canvas wide,
Ready for you to paint your masterpiece, and take your
rightful pride.
So rise up, take control, and create the life you desire,
And show the world that you're capable of achieving
greatness, and setting your soul on fire.

Remember, every great success story began with a fall,
But it's how you rise up that determines your standing
tall.
So don't be afraid to stumble, to falter, or to fail,
For it's in those moments that you'll discover your inner
strength and prevail.

You are a warrior, a survivor, a thriver,
A person of strength, courage, heart, and spirit.
So hold your head high, and never give up the fight,
For you are capable of achieving greatness, and shining
with all your might.

*Keep pushing forward, keep striving to be
The best version of yourself, wild and carefree.
Don't let your past define you, don't let your fears hold
you back,
Keep moving forward, and never look back.*

66. "Rebirth from Ruin"

Sometimes you must destroy to rebuild and renew,
Let go of the old to make way for the true.
The parts of you that are broken, the pieces that are
worn,
Must be torn down to make way for a new form.

Like a phoenix from ashes, you'll rise anew,
From the ruins of your old self, a new you will break
through.
The destruction is painful, the process is slow,
But from the rubble of your past, a brighter future will
grow.

You must let go of fear, doubt, and pain,
To make way for strength, courage, and gain.
The old you must die to make way for the new,
A transformation that's painful, but true.

So don't be afraid to destroy, to tear down and rebuild,

For in the ruins of your old self, a new you will be revealed.
You'll rise from the ashes, like a phoenix born,
A new creation, stronger, wiser, and reborn.

Remember, the darkest night often comes before the dawn,
And the most profound growth comes from the ruins that are torn.
So don't be afraid to face your fears, to let go of the past,
For in the destruction of your old self, a new you will forever last.

You'll emerge from the ashes, like a butterfly from its cocoon,
Transformed, renewed, and reborn, with newfound strength.
Your scars will remain, but they'll no longer define,
For you'll have risen above them, leaving your old self behind.

So let the destruction begin; let the old you fade away,
For in the ruins of your past, a brighter future will be made.
You'll rise from the ashes, like a phoenix born to fly,
A new creation, stronger, wiser, and reborn, with a heart full and high.

67. "The Wise Warrior's Way"

A warrior wise, with strategy keen,
Avoids the battle, its chaos unseen.
He knows that strength lies not in fight,
But in the calm and quiet of night.

He sees the enemy with anger and pride,
But chooses not to engage, to step aside.
For in the heat of battle, wisdom's lost,
And only fools rush in at any cost.

The wise warrior waits with patience and guile,
For the right moment to strike with a gentle smile.
He knows that timing is everything and more,
And that a battle avoided is a victory to store.

His heart is calm, his mind is clear,
He sees the bigger picture and holds it dear.
He knows that war is not the only way
To resolve conflicts and seize the day.

So let us learn from the wise warrior's way,
To avoid the battle and seize a brighter day.
To choose the path of peace and gentle might,
And to emerge victorious in the morning light.

For in the stillness, we find our strength,
And in the silence, our wisdom takes length.
The wise warrior knows that true power lies
Not in aggression, but in gentle, loving eyes.

He walks the path of compassion and understanding too,
And seeks to resolve conflicts with a heart that's true.
He knows that every enemy is a potential friend,
And that love and kindness can be a powerful trend.

So let us follow the wise warrior's lead,
And choose the path of peace with a heart that's freed.
For in the end, it's not the battles we win,
But the love and kindness we share that will forever
spin.

68. "The Search for Purpose"

When purpose is lost and direction unclear,
The mind begins to wander, and distractions draw near.
Like a ship without anchor or a sail without wind,
We drift on the currents of time without a clear mind.

The world outside is loud with its siren's call,
Beckoning us to indulge in its endless thrall.
We chase the fleeting highs of instant gratification,
And fill the void within with temporary fascination.

But like a mirage on the horizon, these distractions
deceive,
Leaving us empty and unfulfilled, our souls to retrieve.
For in the absence of purpose, we're lost and alone,
Adrift in a sea of distractions without a guiding tone.

Yet, within the stillness, a whisper can be heard,
A call to rediscover our heart's deepest word.
A reminder that purpose is not something we find,

But something we cultivate with every choice and every
mind.

So let us quiet the noise and listen to our soul,
And let our purpose emerge like a beacon in control.
For when we're anchored in meaning, distractions lose
their sway,
And we're free to live a life that's authentic every day.

Let us not be seduced by the temptations of the night,
The fleeting pleasures that leave us empty and without
light.
Let us instead seek substance, depth, truth, wisdom,
And cultivate a sense of purpose that will guide us
through life's prism.

For when we're living on purpose, we're living from the
heart,
And our actions and choices are guided by a deeper part.
We're no longer adrift in a sea of distractions and noise,
But instead, we're anchored in a sense of meaning,
purpose, and joys.

So let us seek to live a life that's authentic and true,
A life guided by purpose and a sense of meaning anew.
Let us quiet the noise and listen to our soul,

And let our purpose emerge like a beacon that makes us whole.

69. "Courage in the Face of Fear"

Fear creeps in, like a thief in the night,
Stealing our peace and filling our sight.
It whispers doubts and fills our heart with dread,
A reaction to danger that's instinctively fed.

But courage stands tall, like a beacon of light,
A decision to act in the face of fright.
It's a choice to be brave, to stand and to fight,
To face our fears head-on and shine with all our might.

Fear may be a reaction, but courage is a choice,
A decision to act with a heart that's full of voice.
It's a voice that whispers, "I can and I will",
A voice that echoes, "I'll face my fears and stand still".

So let us choose courage in the face of our fears,
Let us decide to act and wipe away our tears.
For courage is not the absence of fear, but the will to act,
A decision to be brave and to never look back.

*Let us draw on our inner strength and find our heart's
voice,
Let us stand tall and proud and make our courageous
choice.
For in the face of fear, we have two options to take,
To let it consume us or to rise above and make.*

*The choice is ours to make, to choose courage or to hide,
To face our fears with bravery or to let them step inside.
So let us choose to be brave, to stand and to fight,
To face our fears with courage and shine with all our
might.*

*For courage is a muscle that grows with every test,
It's a choice to act with bravery and to always do our
best.
So let us choose courage and make it our guiding light,
And we'll find that we're capable of overcoming any
fright.*

70. "Fear of Losing"

I'm scared of losing you, of watching you walk away
Of being left behind, with nothing to say
I'm scared of the silence, of the emptiness I'd feel
Of the thought of living without you, and the way it
would reveal

My deepest fears, my darkest nights
The thought of losing you haunts my sight
But then I wonder, who's scared of losing me?
Who fears the thought of living without my energy?

Who worries about the emptiness, the silence, and the
pain?
Who's scared of losing me, of watching me walk away in
vain?
I realize that I'm not alone in this fear
That you too may be scared, holding back tears

That we're both scared of losing, of being left behind
But what if we faced this fear and let our love shine?

What if we chose to focus on the love that we share
On the memories we've made, the laughter, and the care?

What if we let go of fear and let our love be strong?
What if we chose to believe that our love will last all life
long?
So let's face this fear together, let's shine a light on our
doubts
Let's choose to focus on love and let our hearts speak out

For I'm not just scared of losing you, I'm scared of losing
me
But with you by my side, I know we'll face eternity
Together we'll brave the storms and weather every test
Our love will be the anchor that holds us strong and best

So let's not let fear consume us, let's not let it win
Let's choose to love each other until the very end
For our love is worth fighting for, it's worth the risk and
the pain
And with you by my side, I know we'll love again and
again.

71. "The Strength of a Smile"

You can't beat someone who smiles at pain,
Who finds strength in the heart's deepest stain.
Their eyes may water, their soul may ache,
But still they'll rise, for their spirit won't break.

Their smile is a shield, a beacon of light,
A defiance of darkness, a refusal to fight.
It's a declaration of hope, a testament of will,
A statement that says, "I'll rise above the pain still."

You can't beat someone who's learned to embrace
The scars that life leaves, the weight of time and space.
They've found a way to heal, to mend, and to repair,
To turn their wounds into wisdom, their pain into
prayer.

Their smile is a reminder that they're still alive,
That they've survived the storms and thrived in the fight.
It's a message of resilience, of courage in the face,

*A declaration that says, "I'll find a way to rise above the
pain's dark place."*

*So don't try to break them, don't try to bring them down,
For they'll just smile at the pain and wear their crown.
For they're the ones who've learned to find strength in
their scars,
And to wear their smile like armor, like a badge of honor
in the stars.*

*They're the ones who've walked through fire and
emerged unbroken,
Who've faced their fears and found a way to awaken.
Their smile is a testament to the strength of their soul,
A declaration that says, "I've been through the storm,
and I'm still whole."*

*So let their smile be a beacon, a guiding light in the dark,
A reminder that we too can rise above the pain and
embark.
On a journey of healing, growth, and might,
Where we can find our own strength and shine with our
own light.*